THE STORY OF THE

ROSE

BOWL

by Tyler Mason

SportsZone
An Imprint of Abdo Publishing | abdopublishing.com

abdopublishing.com

Published by Abdo Publishing, a division of ABDO, PO Box 398166, Minneapolis, Minnesota 55439. Copyright © 2016 by Abdo Consulting Group, Inc. International copyrights reserved in all countries. No part of this book may be reproduced in any form without written permission from the publisher. SportsZone™ is a trademark and logo of Abdo Publishing.

Printed in the United States of America, North Mankato, Minnesota
052015
092015

THIS BOOK CONTAINS
RECYCLED MATERIALS

Cover Photo: Paul Sakuma/AP Images, cover
Interior Photos: Paul Sakuma/AP Images, 1; Marie Appert/Shutterstock Images, 4; AP Images, 7, 8, 10, 12, 14, 15, 16, 24, 27, 42; Max Desfor/AP Images, 18; Collegiate Images/Getty Images, 21, 23; Lance King/Getty Images, 28; Robert Klein/AP Images, 29; Lenny Ignelzi/AP Images, 30; Chris Carlson/AP Images, 32; Kim D. Johnson/AP Images, 33; Matt Sayles/AP Images, 36, 41; Ric Tapia/Icon Sportswire, 38, 39; Doug Sheridan/AP Images, 43

Editor: Patrick Donnelly
Series Designer: Nikki Farinella

Library of Congress Control Number: 2015931669

Cataloging-in-Publication Data
Mason, Tyler.
  The story of the Rose Bowl / Tyler Mason.
    p. cm. -- (Bowl games of college football)
Includes bibliographical references and index.
ISBN 978-1-62403-890-7
1. Rose Bowl (Football game)--History--Juvenile literature. 2. Football--United States--Juvenile literature. 3. College sports--Juvenile literature. I. Title.
796.332--dc23

                                                    2015931669

TABLE OF CONTENTS

1   **Rose Bowl History:**
The Birth of Bowl Games 5

2   **1929: "Wrong-Way" Makes History**
(California vs. Georgia Tech)............... 13

3   **1941: "T" Topples Huskers**
(Stanford vs. Nebraska)......................... 19

4   **1942: Carolina Roses**
(Oregon State vs. Duke) 25

5   **2006: The Vince Young Show**
(Texas vs. USC) 31

6   **2012: Lighting Up the Scoreboard**
(Oregon vs. Wisconsin) 37

Timeline 42
Bowl Records 44
Quotes and Anecdotes............................ 45
Glossary 46
For More Information 47
Index/About the Author......................... 48

The Tournament of Roses Parade is a beloved tradition that dates back to 1890.

ROSE BOWL HISTORY:
THE BIRTH OF BOWL GAMES

Fans call it the "Granddaddy of Them All." The Rose Bowl is the oldest bowl game in college football. It is played every year in Pasadena, California. The first Rose Bowl game was played on January 1, 1902, starting the tradition of bowl games on New Year's Day. Michigan beat Stanford 49–0 in a game that proved to be too lopsided for its own good.

But the Rose Parade came before the Rose Bowl game. The Pasadena Valley Hunt Club founded the parade in 1890 to bring visitors from colder climates to California. Tourists from the Midwest and Northeast United States came to Pasadena to enjoy the warmer weather in the winter. The club's members decorated horse buggies with flowers for the parade.

But it was more than just a parade in 1890. The festivities included games such as tug-of-war, jousting, and foot races. A few years later, the Rose Parade grew bigger. It added parade floats with motors. There were also ostrich races and a race between a camel and an elephant. In 1900, the Rose Parade was shown in movie theaters throughout the country. Once people from other states saw film of the parade, many wanted to travel to California to see it in person.

By 1902, the Tournament of Roses Association was ready to add the emerging sport of football to the festival to attract even more visitors. It wanted to include one team from the West Coast and an opponent from east of the Mississippi River. The University of Southern California (USC) was the closest college football team to Pasadena, but USC did not play an impressive schedule. It played only one game against a college team in 1901, a 6–0 loss to Pomona College. The University of California, Berkeley, was also close to Pasadena, but only two of its nine wins were against college teams.

The association eventually chose Stanford as the team from West Coast. Michigan was its opponent. The first Rose Bowl game was held at the Pasadena town square, which is now called Tournament Park. In 1922,

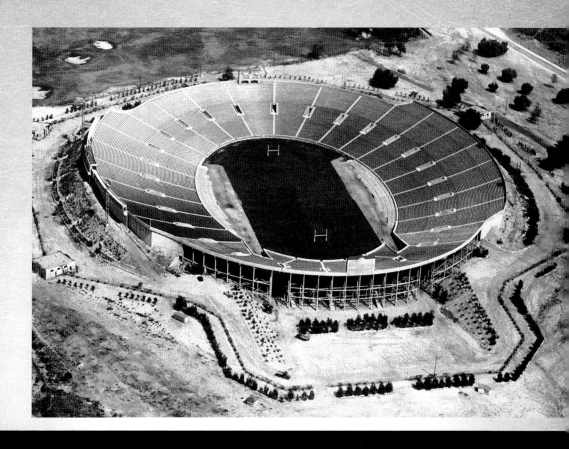

Aerial view of the Rose Bowl Stadium in 1931

a new stadium was built for the football games. It seated 57,000 fans and cost more than $270,000 to build.

The players and coaches from Michigan and Stanford traveled to Pasadena by train for the first game in 1902. It took them almost a week on the train to get to Pasadena.

Michigan had won all 10 of its games before the Rose Bowl and was expected to handle Stanford easily. Michigan had not given up a single point and had scored

Halfback Marshall Goldberg of Pittsburgh, 42, carries the ball during the 1937 Rose Bowl against Washington.

501 points in 10 games. The Wolverines won one of their games 128–0. Stanford won three games that year, lost one, and tied two.

The Rose Bowl result reflected Michigan's dominant season. The forward pass was not legal yet in football, so both teams could only run the ball. Wolverines fullback Neil Snow scored five touchdowns. Running back Willie Heston ran for 170 yards in Michigan's victory.

With eight minutes left in the game, Stanford's captain said his team was too exhausted to continue. Stanford asked for the game to end early, so it did. Michigan was the winner of the first Rose Bowl game.

Because the first Rose Bowl was such a blowout, there wasn't another game for 14 years. The Rose Festival featured other sports to replace football. Competitions included chariot races and polo. Football returned to the Rose Bowl in 1916 when Washington State beat Brown 14–0 at Tournament Park.

Over the years, the Rose Bowl has had many big games and memorable plays. It has also been a part of media history. In 1962, it became the first college bowl game to be televised in color throughout the country. It also was the first college bowl game to draw 100,000 fans. That happened in 1950. In the latter half of the twentieth century, the Big Ten and Pac-10 conferences

Columbia's Cliff Montgomery, *right*, gets off a punt against Stanford in the 1934 Rose Bowl.

each sent a team—usually the conference champion—to the Rose Bowl.

The Rose Parade remains a popular part of the Rose Bowl festivities. The parade floats are still decorated with flowers, but many floats are now more high-tech. Each year, millions of people watch the Rose Parade on television.

During the 2014 season, significant change arrived in the form of a new college football playoff system. The top four teams in the country play in the semifinals at two of six major bowl games, with the winners meeting for the national championship. The Rose Bowl is one of those six bowls, and it hosted the first-ever national semifinal game on January 1, 2015. Second-seeded Oregon set a Rose Bowl scoring record as it defeated number-three Florida State 59–20 to earn a trip to the championship game. Under the new plan, the Rose Bowl will be a national semifinal game once every three years.

POMP AND PAGEANTRY

The Rose Parade tradition began before the Rose Bowl game. The parade route is 5.5 miles (9 km) long and moves at only 2.5 miles per hour (4 km/h). Today, the parade consists of three parts: floats decorated with flowers, marching bands, and horse-riding units.

California's Roy Riegels races toward the end zone in the 1929 Rose Bowl. One

2

1929

"WRONG-WAY" MAKES HISTORY

California vs. Georgia Tech

On January 1, 1929, Georgia Tech squared off against California in the Rose Bowl. It was the only bowl game in college football that season. Georgia Tech entered the game undefeated on the season. California had only one loss.

Back then, most players played on both offense and defense. Roy Riegels played center and linebacker for California. Riegels would be a first-team All-America pick and the Bears' team captain the next season. But in the 1929 Rose Bowl, he made a spectacular blunder that earned him the nickname he would carry the rest of his life: "Wrong-Way" Riegels.

Neither team had put points on the scoreboard yet in the second quarter. Georgia Tech had the ball and hoped

Roy Riegels was a first-team **All-America** center and linebacker for the California Bears.

to score first. Running back Stumpy Thomason ran the ball for 6 yards on the first play of the drive. However, Thomason fumbled the ball at the end of his run.

Riegels picked up the fumble at Georgia Tech's 34-yard line and started running. There was a problem, though. He was running in the wrong direction. Riegels sprinted down the sideline toward the California end zone. California defensive back Benny Lom chased after Riegels and finally caught his teammate near the goal line. But before he could head back the other way, Riegels was tackled by a horde of Georgia Tech players at the 1-yard line.

Roy Riegels is chased by his California teammates as he runs the wrong way with a fumble in the 1929 Rose Bowl.

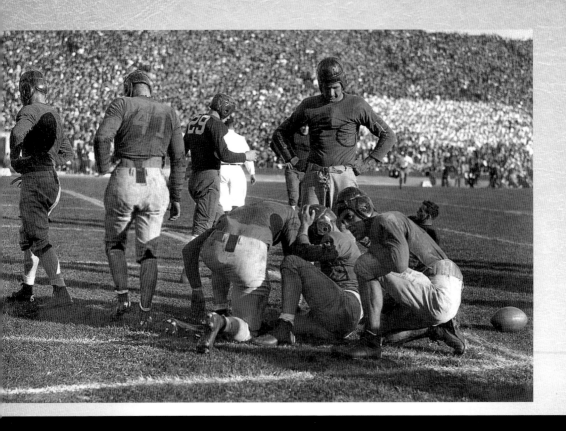

Roy Riegels, *seated*, holds his head in his hands surrounded by his dejected teammates after California's star center ran the wrong way with a fumble in the 1929 Rose Bowl.

Rather than risking a play on offense from its own 1-yard line, California punted on the next play. Lom was the punter and Riegels was the long snapper. But Georgia Tech's Vance Maree blocked the punt for a safety. California trailed 2–0 thanks to "Wrong Way" Riegels's mistake.

Those two points proved to be crucial. Georgia Tech led 8–0 after Thomason scored a 15-yard touchdown. California scored in the fourth quarter on a touchdown pass by Lom to make it 8–7. But that touchdown was not enough—Georgia Tech won 8–7. The safety after Riegels's run was the difference in the game.

"I didn't realize [my error] until Benny Lom chased me down the field and said I was going the wrong way," Riegels said. "He grabbed my arm and started pulling me down."

Riegels played a good game other than his one mistake. He even blocked a Georgia Tech punt in the second half. He also went on to coach after his playing career ended and later joined the Air Force. Despite all of that, he is still remembered for his wrong-way run.

Riegels was enshrined in the Rose Bowl Hall of Fame in 1991 and died two years later. His error in the 1929 game remains one of the most famous plays in college football history.

ROSE BOWL GROWTH

The current Rose Bowl Stadium was built in 1922. It was expanded in 1928 to seat 76,000. In 1949, 1950, and 1972, more seats were added. After many renovations, the Rose Bowl Stadium now holds 92,542 fans. It has been the home of University of California, Los Angeles (UCLA) football since 1982. The expansion was vital to the Rose Bowl hosting five Super Bowls between 1977 and 1993, as well as the World Cup and Women's World Cup soccer tournaments.

Clark Shaughnessy, center, the architect of the T formation

3

1941
"T" TOPPLES HUSKERS
Stanford vs. Nebraska

Fans at the 1941 Rose Bowl got a glimpse of the future, thanks to the success of an innovative offense that soon became wildly popular throughout the football world.

That game featured an undefeated Stanford team against the Nebraska Cornhuskers. Stanford had won only one game the year before. New coach Clark Shaughnessy had a solution to make his team better. He introduced the T formation to the Stanford offense. Only a few schools were using it at that time. Stanford was running a single-wing offense before switching to the T formation. In the single-wing formation, the center snapped the ball directly to a running back.

The ball carrier would then follow the other backs blocking for him.

The T formation was different from anything Stanford's players had run before. It included a quarterback and three running backs. The quarterback's main job was to pass the football or hand it to a running back. Two of the three backs were mainly runners. The other one was primarily there to catch passes.

Nebraska had to gear its practices to defend the T formation. The Cornhuskers had not yet faced this new formation. They watched film of a Stanford game to prepare for the new offense. Nebraska practiced outside with temperatures near freezing. Eventually the weather forced the Cornhuskers to head to Arizona to practice before the game.

All of Nebraska's preparation was not enough. On January 1, 1941, Stanford executed the T formation to perfection. Frankie Albert led the way at quarterback, with Hugh Gallarneau and Pete Kmetovic at halfback, and Norm Standlee at fullback.

It was the Cornhuskers who struck first, though. Nebraska fullback Vike Francis scored on a short touchdown run for a 7–0 Huskers lead. The touchdown came only six plays into the game.

STANFORD

NEBRASKA

ROSE BOWL, JANUARY 1, 1941

PASADENA, CALIFORNIA

$.243 SELLIN
.007 SALES
TOTAL PRICE 25 CENTS

The cover of the program for the 1941 Rose Bowl between Stanford and Nebraska.

Stanford answered with a touchdown of its own. Using the T formation, Gallarneau ran for a 9-yard touchdown to tie the game in the first quarter. The scoring was back and forth after that. Nebraska quarterback Herm Rohrig connected for a 33-yard touchdown pass to Allen Zikmund. Stanford blocked the extra point, so Nebraska led 13–7. But the T formation worked again for Stanford, this time as Albert found Gallarneau open for a 41-yard touchdown pass. Gallarneau caught the ball near the 10-yard line and sprinted into the end zone. That gave Stanford a 14–13 lead at the half.

But Stanford did not rely only on its offense that day. Its special teams turned in one of the biggest plays of the game. In the third quarter, Kmetovic returned a punt 39 yards for a touchdown. Kmetovic also rushed for 141

WEST MEETS MIDWEST

The Rose Bowl changed in 1946. The Big 9 (now the Big Ten) signed an agreement to send its champion to Pasadena to play a team from the Pacific Coast Conference (PCC). The first game after this agreement was in 1947 between Michigan and USC. The agreement was modified in 1960 when the PCC split up. Many of its teams formed the new Athletic Association of Western Universities, which eventually became today's Pac-12 Conference. The Big Ten agreed to continue sending its champion to the Rose Bowl to face the winner of the western conference. It remains the oldest agreement of its kind between two major conferences.

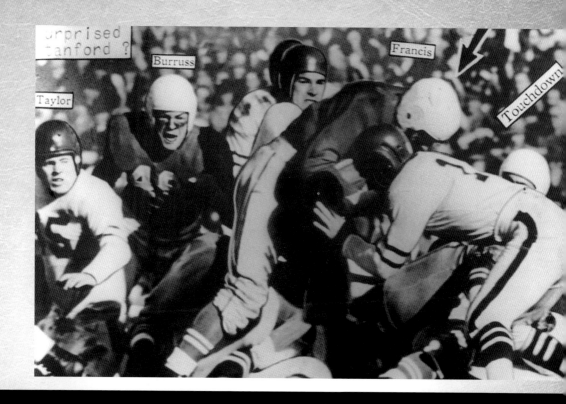

surprised
Stanford ?

Taylor

Burruss

Francis

Touchdown

Nebraska fullback Vike Francis bowls through the Stanford defense to score the first touchdown of the day at the 1941 Rose Bowl.

yards in the game. His punt return provided the final points of the game, as Stanford held on to win 21–13. Stanford's backs combined to rush for 254 yards against Nebraska's defense.

The T formation was such a success in the Rose Bowl that Shaughnessy made a bold prediction after Stanford's win. He said that the T formation would become popular in college football, and his prediction was right. Within 10 years, approximately 250 college football teams were using it.

Duke captain Bob Barnett, *left*, and head coach Wallace Wade prepare for the 1942 Rose Bowl against Oregon State.

4

1942
CAROLINA ROSES
Oregon State vs. Duke

Only one game in Rose Bowl history was not played in Pasadena. That was in 1942, when the game was moved to North Carolina because of World War II (1939–1945).

On December 7, 1941, Japanese airplanes bombed the US naval base at Pearl Harbor in Honolulu, Hawaii. The United States declared war on Japan the next day, thrusting it into a conflict that had been raging around the globe. The attack on Pearl Harbor put the immediate future of the Rose Bowl and the Rose Parade in doubt. Government officials discouraged any events that might draw large crowds to the West Coast. They feared that if the Japanese planes could reach Hawaii, they might be able to reach the mainland as well. And with 1 million spectators watching the Rose Parade and 90,000 fans at the Rose Bowl game, Pasadena would be a likely target.

The matchup for the Rose Bowl had been set on December 1. The PCC champion Oregon State Beavers were to face the Duke Blue Devils. After the Pearl Harbor attack, Rose Bowl officials scrambled to find a new site to play the game. Officials from Chicago said the city could host the game at Soldier Field. Duke head coach Wallace Wade said his team could host the game in Durham, North Carolina. Eventually the game was moved to Duke Stadium in Durham. Temporary seating was added to expand the capacity from 35,000 to 56,000 fans.

The selection of the new site provided a challenge for Oregon State. The Beavers took a train more than 3,000 miles (4,800 km) from Corvallis, Oregon, to North Carolina. On the five-day trip, the team stopped in three different cities to practice.

Early in the season, Oregon State struggled to get the upper hand in the PCC. The Beavers were 2–2 after four games, but they went on a winning streak that included an upset over the reigning Rose Bowl champion. They shut down Stanford's mighty T formation in a 10–0 victory. The Beavers beat Oregon in their final game to clinch the PCC title and earn a trip to the Rose Bowl.

A patriotic rally in New York City captures the spirit of the country on December 27, 1941, five days before the 1942 Rose Bowl. The game was moved to Durham, North Carolina, because government officials feared a possible attack on the West Coast.

Meanwhile, Duke was a perfect 9-0 during the regular season. The Blue Devils were ranked number two in the nation behind Minnesota. However, the Golden Gophers could not play in the Rose Bowl because at that time the Western Conference (which later became the Big Ten) did not allow its teams to play in bowl games. That gave Duke the chance to accept a Rose Bowl invitation.

The game itself was a close one. The Blue Devils were favored to win but fell behind early. Oregon State scored first on a 15-yard run by Don Durdan in the

Duke Stadium—since renamed Wallace Wade Stadium in honor of the legendary coach—was the site of the only Rose Bowl played outside of Pasadena, California.

first quarter. Duke responded with a touchdown in the second quarter for a 7–7 tie at halftime.

The Beavers and Blue Devils traded scores in the third quarter. George Zellick caught a 31-yard touchdown pass from Oregon State quarterback Bob Dethman. Duke tied the game on a 1-yard run by Winston Siegfried.

Oregon State took the lead for good on a 68-yard touchdown reception by Gene Gray. Duke managed a safety in the fourth quarter but the Beavers held on to win 20–16.

Many players from that game went on to fight in World War II. Oregon State's Gray joined the Army Air Forces and flew planes over Germany. His teammate Zellick enlisted in the US Marine Corps shortly after returning to Oregon. Duke captain Bob Barnett also joined the marines three weeks after the Rose Bowl.

The Rose Bowl returned to California in 1943 when Georgia faced UCLA. The game in 1942 remains the only time the Rose Bowl has been played outside of Pasadena.

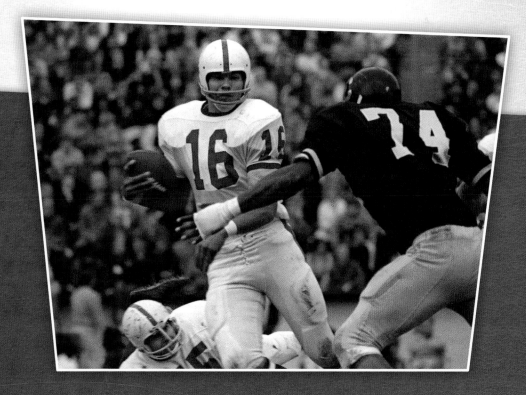

HALL OF FAME

More than 100 players, coaches, and broadcasters have been inducted into the Rose Bowl Hall of Fame. The first class was named in 1989. The first four inductees were Bump Elliott (Michigan), Woody Hayes (Ohio State), Howard Jones (USC), and Jim Plunkett (Stanford), *above*. Other notable players in the Rose Bowl Hall of Fame include Bob Griese (Purdue), O. J. Simpson (USC), Dick Butkus (Illinois), Warren Moon (Washington), and Ron Dayne (Wisconsin).

USC tailback Reggie Bush fights for extra yardage against Texas in the 2006 Rose Bowl.

5

2006
THE VINCE YOUNG SHOW
Texas vs. USC

A fter more than a half century featuring only teams from the current Big Ten and Pac-12 conferences, the Rose Bowl entered a new era. In 1997 college football created the Bowl Championship Series (BCS) to determine its national champion. The Rose Bowl became one of four bowls that would host the national title game every fourth year, no matter which conferences the top two teams played in. It also meant that the Big Ten and Pac-12 champions could be sent to different bowls.

Traditionalists were not pleased, but the change did open the Rose Bowl to storied programs that had not been eligible to play in Pasadena since the 1940s. One of those teams was the Texas Longhorns. The longtime

USC quarterback Matt Leinart airs one out against Texas in the 2006 Rose Bowl.

powerhouse from the Big 12 made its Rose Bowl debut in January 2005 with a win against Michigan. One year later, the Longhorns were back for an even better Rose Bowl game against USC.

The 2006 Rose Bowl also was the national championship game. The Trojans were ranked number one in the country, and Texas was number two. The teams had been atop the national rankings since the season started, and the excitement grew throughout that autumn as fans began to anticipate a matchup of the two best teams in the country. The game certainly lived up to the hype surrounding it.

Texas defenders Michael Huff, *left*, and Brian Robison, *center*, celebrate after stopping LenDale White, *right*, short on a key fourth-down play late in the 2006 Rose Bowl.

The two most recent winners of the Heisman Trophy, given to the nation's best college football player, lined up for USC. Quarterback Matt Leinart won it in 2004 as a junior when he led the Trojans to the national title. He came back the next season and led USC to a 12–0 record, but Trojans running back Reggie Bush won the Heisman. As a former Heisman winner, Leinart was eligible to participate in the voting. Even he voted for

Bush, who led the nation with 2,218 total yards from scrimmage that year. Leinart finished third in the voting, one spot behind Texas quarterback Vince Young.

Young knew he had a chance not only to win a national championship for Texas, but to show he was the best player in college football that year. He took that chance and ran with it—literally. Young rushed for 200 yards and three touchdowns against USC, and he added 267 passing yards as well.

Young stole the show that night, but Leinart had a good game for USC. He completed 29 of 40 passes for 365 yards. Leinart also threw a 22-yard touchdown to Dwayne Jarrett in the fourth quarter. That touchdown pass gave USC a 38–26 lead with 6:42 to play in the game.

Then Young took over for the Longhorns. He completed five passes for 44 yards on Texas' next drive. Young then scored on a 17-yard touchdown run with 4:03 remaining. That cut USC's lead to 38–33.

The Longhorns defense then came up with a big play on fourth down. USC had the ball at its own 45-yard line and needed two yards to earn another set of downs. But the Texas line stuffed Trojans running back LenDale White for a 1-yard gain. Texas got the ball back with 2:13 to play needing a touchdown to win.

Young's heroics continued. He threw for 31 yards and rushed for 12 more to get the ball to USC's 8-yard line. On fourth-and-five, Young scooted around the right end for an 8-yard touchdown to give the Longhorns a 39–38 lead. Texas also scored on the two-point conversion to lead 41–38 with only 19 seconds remaining.

USC ran only two more plays before the game was over. Young and the Longhorns had come back to win the 2006 Rose Bowl and the national championship. The loss snapped the Trojans' 34-game winning streak. It was Texas' first national championship since 1970. Young was named the game's Most Valuable Player.

The game became an instant classic, but USC's participation was eventually wiped from the history books. In 2011, Bush was ruled ineligible during the 2004 season for receiving illegal payments. Bush also had to give up his Heisman Trophy.

PASS THE BEEF

In the week leading up to the Rose Bowl, players from both teams take part in the Lawry's Beef Bowl. The teams compete to see who can eat the most prime rib at Lawry's Restaurant in Beverly Hills, California. The individual record is believed to be held by former Michigan offensive lineman Ed Muransky. He downed 8 pounds (3.6 kg) of beef in 1978.

Wisconsin quarterback Russell Wilson scrambles for extra yards against Oregon in the 2012 Rose Bowl.

6

2012
LIGHTING UP
THE SCOREBOARD

Oregon vs. Wisconsin

The University of Oregon had not won the Rose Bowl since 1917. That changed in 2012 when the Ducks won a shootout against Wisconsin that fans will not soon forget.

The scoring went back and forth for most of the game as neither team could stop the other. Wisconsin scored first on a 38-yard pass from quarterback Russell Wilson to wide receiver Jared Abbrederis. Oregon answered quickly with a 1-yard touchdown run by LaMichael James. Wilson ran in a 4-yard touchdown less than four minutes later. But the Ducks responded again. This time it was freshman running back De'Anthony Thomas scoring on a 91-yard run, the longest in

Oregon running back De'Anthony Thomas streaks down the sideline for a long gain in the 2012 Rose Bowl.

Rose Bowl history. Thomas's run made it 14–14 after the first quarter.

Wisconsin running back Montee Ball's thirty-ninth touchdown of the season put the Badgers back on top 21–14. Oregon returned the kickoff almost to midfield. One play later Oregon tied the game on a 54-yard pass from Darron Thomas to Kenjon Barner.

Each team scored another touchdown before halftime. Wisconsin defensive end Louis Nzegwu returned a fumble 33 yards to the end zone. That gave the Badgers a 28–21 lead. Just before halftime, Oregon wide receiver Lavasier Tuinei caught a 3-yard

Wisconsin running back Montee Ball tied the single-season touchdown record with a second-quarter score in the 2012 Rose Bowl.

touchdown pass from Darron Thomas. The teams headed to the locker room tied 28–28.

The Ducks took the lead early in the third quarter. De'Anthony Thomas scored on another long run. His second touchdown of the game went for 64 yards and put Oregon up 35–28. Wisconsin wasn't finished, though. The Badgers added a field goal and then a touchdown in the third quarter on a pass from Wilson to receiver Nick Toon to regain the lead, 38–35.

But then Wisconsin's offense hit the wall. The Badgers did not score in the fourth quarter, and the Ducks came back for the win. Oregon scored the go-ahead touchdown on a catch by Tuinei and took a seven-point lead after a field goal.

Wisconsin had a chance to tie the game in the final minute. The Badgers got the ball back at their own 13-yard line with 16 seconds to play and no timeouts left. Wilson completed passes to Abbrederis and Toon to move the ball to Oregon's 25-yard line. Wilson then tried to stop the clock by spiking the ball, but time expired. Oregon won 45–38.

The 83 points scored were the most in Rose Bowl history. That was only one of many records set in this game. Ball tied Oklahoma State's Barry Sanders for the most touchdowns in a single season. Wisconsin and Oregon scored 56 total points in the first half. That was the most points in a half in Rose Bowl history. The old record of 45 was set in 1999 by Wisconsin and UCLA. The 28 points in the first quarter were also a Rose Bowl record.

BADGER COMEBACK FALLS SHORT

Wisconsin played in another memorable, high-scoring Rose Bowl. In 1963 the second-ranked Badgers faced number one USC in a showdown for the national championship. Wisconsin fell behind 42–14, but quarterback Ron Vander Kelen almost pulled off an amazing comeback. The Badgers scored the last 23 points, but the Trojans recovered an onside kick to seal a 42–37 victory. Vander Kelen set Rose Bowl records with 33 completions and 401 passing yards.

Oregon's Darron Thomas, *left*, and Lavasier Tuinei leap over a fallen Marcus Cromartie of Wisconsin after an Oregon touchdown in the 2012 Rose Bowl.

TIMELINE

1890
The Tournament of Roses Parade is held for the first time.

1902
The first Rose Bowl game is played at Tournament Park as Michigan beats Stanford 49–0.

1904
Chariot races replace football at Tournament Park.

1916
Football returns to Pasadena when Washington State beats Brown 14–0 in the Rose Bowl.

1922
Construction on the Rose Bowl Stadium is completed. The new stadium seats 57,000.

1926
The Rose Bowl is broadcast on local radio for the first time.

1942
World War II forces the Rose Bowl to move to Durham, North Carolina. However, the visiting Oregon State Beavers still beat Duke 20–16.

1946
The Rose Bowl agreement between the Big Ten and Pacific Coast Conference begins.

1947
The Rose Bowl game and Rose Parade are televised locally for the first time.

1950
After a stadium expansion, the Rose Bowl becomes the first bowl game to draw 100,000 fans.

1963

Wisconsin quarterback Ron Vander Kelen sets new Rose Bowl records for passing yards (401), pass attempts (48), and completions (33) in a loss to USC.

1968

For the first time, the Rose Bowl is broadcast live around the world via satellite.

1977

The Rose Bowl Stadium plays host to its first Super Bowl. The Oakland Raiders beat the Minnesota Vikings 32–14.

1980

USC running back and Heisman Trophy winner Charles White sets a Rose Bowl record with 247 rushing yards.

1990

Michigan's Bo Schembechler coaches in his tenth and final Rose Bowl, more than any other coach.

2006

Texas quarterback Vince Young gains a record 467 yards of total offense to help the Longhorns beat USC 41–38 and win the national title.

2012

Oregon beats Wisconsin 45–38 in the highest-scoring game in Rose Bowl history.

2014

The 100th Rose Bowl Game is played. Michigan State defeats Stanford 24–20.

2015

Oregon beats Florida State 59–20 in the semifinals of a new four-team college football playoff.

BOWL RECORDS

Most total yards, team
639, Oregon vs. Florida State, 2015

Most total yards, individual
467, Vince Young, Texas vs. USC, 2006

Most passing yards
456, Danny O'Neil, Oregon vs. Penn State, 1995

Most rushing yards
247, Charles White, USC vs. Ohio State, 1980

Most rushing touchdowns
5, Neil Snow, Michigan vs. Stanford, 1902

Longest touchdown run
91 yards, De'Anthony Thomas, Oregon vs. Wisconsin, 2012

Longest touchdown reception
76 yards, Curt Stephenson, Michigan vs. Washington, 1978

Longest field goal
52 yards, Rob Houghtlin, Iowa vs. UCLA, 1986

Most points scored, one team
59, Oregon vs. Florida State, 2015

Most combined points scored
83, Oregon vs. Wisconsin, 2012

Most tackles
17, Percy Snow, Michigan State vs. USC, 1988; and John Boyett, Oregon vs. Wisconsin, 2012

Longest kickoff return
103 yards, Al Hoisch, UCLA vs. Illinois, 1947

Most appearances
33, USC

Most victories
24, USC

*through the 2015 Rose Bowl

QUOTES AND ANECDOTES

"What am I seeing? What's wrong with me? Am I crazy? Am I crazy? Am I crazy?"—radio broadcaster Graham McNamee, reacting to California's Roy Riegels running the wrong way with a fumble in the 1929 Rose Bowl

"I go into the Air Service January 24, and if I get killed, I can take it now and die happy. That's how you feel when you win a Rose Bowl football game."—Oregon State captain Martin Chaves after beating Duke in the 1942 Rose Bowl game that was moved because of World War II

Michigan coach Bo Schembechler coached 10 Wolverines teams that played in the Rose Bowl, but the legendary coach was not on the sideline for his first trip to Pasadena. He suffered a heart attack the night before the Rose Bowl on January 1, 1970, forcing him to miss the game. Michigan lost to USC 10-3.

"I'm kind of tired of tears of sadness. I wanted to come out here and experience tears of joy at some point."—Wisconsin head coach Bret Bielema, whose teams lost back-to-back close games in the 2011 and 2012 Rose Bowls.

"It's a classy bowl. Everything around is so much fun. It's still exciting for us in every way. I think it's different for the Big Ten because they're leaving part of the country to come to Hollywood."—USC coach Pete Carroll before the 2009 Rose Bowl

"The stadium is a packed stadium on that day, and the emotions are high; it is extra special. When you play there, in that game, you become a part of history."—Washington Huskies wide receiver Todd Elstrom, who played in the 2001 Rose Bowl

GLOSSARY

conference

A group of schools that join to create a league for their sports teams. The Big Ten Conference and Pac-12 Conference are examples.

freshman

A first-year college student.

fullback

An offensive player who sometimes runs with the football but is also responsible for blocking.

fumble

When a player with the ball loses possession, allowing the defense the opportunity to recover it.

Heisman Trophy

The award given yearly to the best player in college football.

onside kick

A kickoff that is purposely short with the hope that the kicking team can recover the ball.

safety

When a player is tackled in his own end zone, giving the opposing team two points.

special teams

The players on the field for kicking and punting plays.

T formation

A type of offense that uses three running backs plus a quarterback.

FOR MORE INFORMATION

Further Reading

Beck, Stan, and Jack Wilkinson. *College Sports Traditions: Picking Up Butch, Silent Night, and Hundreds of Others*. Lanham, MD: Scarecrow Press, Inc., 2013.

Curtis, Brian. "War and Roses: The 1942 Rose Bowl rallied a rattled country." *Sports Illustrated*, Aug. 14, 2013.

Eisenhammer, Fred, and Eric B. Sondheimer. *College Football's Most Memorable Games*. Jefferson, NC: McFarland & Company, 2010.

Wilner, Barry. *USC Trojans*. Minneapolis, MN: Abdo Publishing, 2013.

Websites

To learn more about Bowl Games of College Football, visit **booklinks.abdopublishing.com**. These links are routinely monitored and updated to provide the most current information available.

Place to Visit

College Football Hall of Fame
250 Marietta Street NW
Atlanta, Georgia 30313
404-880-4800
www.cfbhall.com
This hall of fame and museum highlights the greatest players and moments in the history of college football. Relocated from South Bend, Indiana, in 2014, it includes multiple galleries, a theater, and an interactive area where fans can test their football skills.

INDEX

Abbrederis, Jared, 37, 40
Albert, Frankie, 20, 22

Ball, Montee, 38, 40
Barner, Kenjon, 38
Barnett, Bob, 29
Bush, Reggie, 33–34, 35
Butkus, Dick, 29

Dayne, Ron, 29
Dethman, Bob, 28
Durdan, Don, 27

Elliott, Bump, 29

Francis, Vike, 20

Gallarneau, Hugh, 20, 22
Gray, Gene, 28
Griese, Bob, 29

Hayes, Woody, 29
Heston, Willie, 9

James, LaMichael, 37
Jarrett, Dwayne, 34
Jones, Howard, 29

Kmetovic, Pete, 20, 22–23

Leinart, Matt, 33–34
Lom, Benny, 14, 16–17

Maree, Vance, 16
Moon, Warren, 29
Muransky, Ed, 35

Nzegwu, Louis, 38

Plunkett, Jim, 29

Riegels, Roy, 13–14, 16–17
Rohrig, Herm, 22

Sanders, Barry, 40
Shaughnessy, Clark, 19, 23

Siegfried, Winston, 28
Simpson, O. J., 29
Snow, Neil, 9

Thomas, Darron, 38–39
Thomas, De'Anthony, 37–39
Thomason, Stumpy, 14, 16
Toon, Nick, 39, 40
Tuinei, Lavasier, 38, 40

Vander Kelen, Ron, 40

Wade, Wallace, 26
White, LenDale, 34
Wilson, Russell, 37, 39–40

Young, Vince, 34–35

Zellick, George, 28
Zikmund, Allen, 22

About the Author

Tyler Mason studied journalism at the University of Wisconsin–Madison, where he was named the 2008 Big Ten Conference William R. Reed Memorial Award winner. He has covered professional and college sports in Minneapolis and St. Paul, Minnesota, since 2009. He lives in Hudson, Wisconsin, with his wife.